SING WITH PRAISE

Sing With Praise

❄

Thora Hird
with Liz Barr

Fount
An Imprint of HarperCollinsPublishers

Dedicated to Cecil Jackson-Cole
1901–1979
Founder of Help the Aged

Fount Paperbacks is an Imprint of
HarperCollins*Religious*
Part of HarperCollins*Publishers*
77–85 Fulham Palace Road, London W6 8JB

First published in Great Britain
in 1995 by Fount Paperbacks

1 3 5 7 9 10 8 6 4 2

A catalogue record for this book is
available from the British Library

ISBN 0 00627 9619

Printed and bound in Great Britain by
HarperCollinsManufacturing Glasgow

Contents

Foreword

I am glad to commend this little book.

It will give its readers many a chuckle, as it has done for me. Would we expect any other reaction when Dame Thora Hird, popular presenter for so long of *Praise Be* and other radio and television programmes, has been a major contributor?

The book will do more than make us chuckle. It will make us *think*. For within the contents of a humorous book, many of the big issues of life, of suffering, of old age are faced and faced openly and honestly. Some readers might like to keep this book by their bedside and when sleeplessness makes the night seem intolerably long, dip into it. Like Little Jack Horner eating his Christmas Pie, they may put in their thumb and take out a plum – and enjoy it! Not all the hymns would pass examination by the Poet Laureate, nor all the prayers by the Liturgical Commission. But that is not the point. They give expression to realities deeply experienced and the writers invite the readers to share those realities with them.

Best of all, this book will help readers to *pray*. 'One deep calls to another', and the various contributions will lead many to enter into communion with the Lord who is close to those who suffer and who had to endure some of the afflictions that flesh is heir to. I am sure that Dame Thora Hird will agree with me in inviting you, as you dip into this book, to chuckle, to think and to pray – all worthwhile activities.

Donald Coggan, Vice President of Help the Aged

Preface

> I tell you, whenever you did this for one of
> the least important of these brothers of
> mine, you did it for me.
>
> *(Matthew 25:40)*

It was reading this sentence of Our Lord that inspired
Christian businessman Cecil Jackson-Cole to set up a
small charity called Voluntary and Christian Service in
the late 1950s.

Operating from a corner of his premises in the
Strand, he served the needs of people less fortunate
than himself. From this, Help the Aged developed,
initially as a charity for elderly refugees, but subse-
quently expanding to serve the needs of all older
people, both at home and overseas.

Now, more than thirty years on, Help the Aged ranks
eighth in terms of voluntary income in the UK. It works
to improve the quality of life of elderly people both in
the UK and internationally, particularly those who are
frail, isolated or poor.

Help the Aged in the UK campaigns through
vigorous fundraising and partnerships with industry,
business and government at local, national and international levels. It also works with schools, groups and
other charities. Help the Aged provides housing
schemes, campaigns for greater safety in the home,
makes grants for community initiatives such as trans-
port and is a prime provider of information and advice,
not least via SeniorLine, the only free national
telephone helpline for elderly people and their carers.

Help the Aged's commitment to partnership

is also present in a global perspective through its contribution to HelpAge International programmes. It is a leading member of HelpAge International, an organization which Help the Aged founded in 1983, and represents a network of 45 independent, non-governmental organizations from four continents, working with and for disadvantaged older people worldwide to achieve a lasting improvement in the quality of their lives.

Funds used internationally support such projects as primary health care, ophthalmic programmes, training, income generation schemes, aid for refugees and disaster relief. A total of 54 countries worldwide benefit from Help the Aged advice, training and support.

Building on its religious background Help the Aged has developed into a successful crusade, helping millions of elderly people at home and overseas.

> By learning more about the needs and gifts
> of the World's elderly, by affirming the full
> dignity of persons in later life, the churches
> will discover more completely their own
> calling.

Thus wrote Susanne and James Paul in *Humanity Comes of Age*[1] published in 1994 by the World Council of Churches in Geneva. Help the Aged is playing its part in thus educating churches by having established a National Sunday for Elderly People – held annually on the Sunday nearest to the UN International Day for Elderly People, 1st October. The charity produces a pack of ideas to help churches plan their worship on that day and holds special services in London and various other parts of the UK to show churches of all

[1] Available from Interchurch House, 35 Lower Marsh, London SE1 7RL

denominations just what they might also be doing.

The first of such services was held in 1992 at St James's Church in Clerkenwell, London. The Archbishop of York, then Bishop of London, attended and gave the address. The following year was European Year for Older People. It was suggested that older people be asked to write a hymn for use at services for National Sunday for Elderly People. Consequently a short note appeared in the monthly magazine *Yours* and the quarterly publication *The Reader*. The response was 200 new hymns from 120 composers! That year Help the Aged held two special services – one at Westminster Cathedral and the other at Londonderry Cathedral in Northern Ireland. At Westminster, Joan Bartlett's 'Inspire in us' was used (see page 13) and in Derry, Ruth Dunston's 'God the Father' (see page 76). Ruth's hymn was also broadcast by BBC Devon during their morning service on National Sunday for Elderly People.

Theo Jackson-Cole, the widow of the founder of Help the Aged, suggested that we might possibly use more of the hymns for a special hymn book, so the idea for this book was born. Thora Hird is a long-standing friend of Help the Aged and founder member of SAGE (Stage for Age), the charity's Celebrity Support Committee. She attended Help the Aged's special Epiphany service in January 1995 and was introduced to this project. The book had become something more than an idea! Thora selected 45 of the hymns from 31 different writers and the result is *Sing with Praise*.

In 1995 Help the Aged had two special services on National Sunday for Elderly People. In London Lord Coggan, former Archbishop of Canterbury, preached in Westminster Abbey. The Venerable John Delight, former Archdeacon of Stoke, preached in Lichfield Cathedral in the Midlands. *Sing with Praise* was launched at both and hymns from the book were sung.

I hope that more and more churches will use this book to help them 'more fully to discover their own calling'. And in remembering older people they will remember the work of Help the Aged, remember the Charity in their prayers and in their giving – caring for older people as they deserve to be cared for is a costly business. I wish you great joy in singing (or even just reading) these beautiful lines from the pens of senior citizens up and down the country.

Peter Bowring, President of Help the Aged

1

The best is yet to be!

> Grow old along with me!
> The best is yet to be . . .
> *(Robert Browning: Rabbi ben Ezra)*

> God give me work
> Till my life shall end –
> And life
> Till my work is done.
> *(On the tomb of Winifred Holtby,*
> *Christian novelist, d. 1935)*

That's my prayer, too: 'God give me work till my life shall end . . .' Next to my bed I have a little framed saying, and it's the first thing I see every morning, and it says:

> Don't stop doing things because you're growing old –
> you only grow old if you stop doing things.

Somebody sent it to me, and I'm very grateful, because I think it's so *true*. I can honestly say that I have never really felt old. Now I know it's very easy for someone like me to say that, and it isn't always just that easy *not* to feel old, especially when you're poorly. I have been blessed with fairly good health, well, very good health, apart from arthritis, where I've walked with a stick since 1972. But the thing that has helped me most from *feeling* old is the fact that I have been able to keep on working – and, praise the Lord, I'm still working, and I've always been so grateful for that. I could stop. Let us be honest. I don't have to work another day in my life, but that wouldn't do for me. I always say to people who say to me: 'Oo, Thora, I do wish you wouldn't take on so much!' 'Why? Do you want me to die?' Because for me, that is the thing I am most afraid of, not being able to work. And the Lord has always been very good to me in this respect, however much pain I may be in – and anybody with arthritis knows how much that is – the minute I start working it disappears, just for as long as takes me to do whatever is necessary – stand up and speak after a lunch, give an interview, act in a scene, walk a few steps in a play without my stick, or whatever it is I have to do, I can do it, and the pain disappears. Whoosh – it comes back the minute I stop, of course! But I always say to the Lord 'I won't complain about any of the pain I get when I'm not working, if you take it away when I do.' And we both keep our side of the bargain!

For a short while this last spring, though, I thought that my working days might be over. I was down in the country, where I have a cottage, and all of a sudden I put my foot on the floor and – whoohoosh! – I've never known such pain in my life. I really have not. Jan, my daughter, said, 'What's the matter?' And I said, 'I can't get up.' It was a Monday afternoon and she rang my doctor in London, and he said, 'Can you get her here for seven o'clock?' Well, it's a two-hour drive. She packed my house up, put all the food in the car, she's so good, and we got there for seven o'clock. The doctor examined me and he said, 'Well, this is a hospital job.' I said, 'When? Tomorrow?' And he said 'Tonight. I'm sending for the ambulance.' So I never even got back to my own house in London. I went straight from the country to the doctor's, and then straight to the hospital.

I've had my right hip replaced twice, which is as much as any surgeon wants to do, but this time it wasn't the hip, it was the bone from the knee to the hip that had gone to sort of powder. So I've got a metal piece there now. I can't tell. Surgeons are such brilliant people. When they come round to your bed – and anybody reading this knows what it's like, if you've been in hospital – it's a royal visitation. Mine said, 'You see, Mrs Scott, it isn't usual for us to cure a lady of 83 . . .' and here he paused dramatically . . . 'to go back to work!'

So I didn't say anything. No, I didn't, because I knew he was right, in a way. It was a four-hour operation, and I was 83, so let's put it like that. But I didn't like it. And about two mornings afterwards he came round again with another surgeon, and he said had I any pain? and I said, 'Well, it's a little bit painful, but no, I'm really doing marvellously.' And he said, 'I should think you are! You see, we aren't used to curing people of 83 . . .' (dramatic pause for effect) '. . . so that they can go back to work!' So I didn't say anything again, because I wouldn't be rude to this brilliant man, with the other surgeon and all the nurses fluttering round him. But the third time he came round he had a set of students, and he was on about one thing and another that I'd had done, for their benefit, and then he turned to me and he said, 'You see, Mrs Scott . . .'and I held up my hand and said, 'Don't say it! Please!' He said, 'Say what?' 'That you are not used to curing people of 83 . . . to go back to work!' And he laughed, I will say. I didn't mean to be rude, but I thought, 'If he says that every time he comes round . . .' Because I had every intention of going back to work, you see. It was what was keeping me going.

Of course, when I say 'work', it doesn't have to mean having a job. Acting happens to be the kind of job you can go on doing long after normal retirement age – if anyone will have you! But many of the 'young' oldies I meet keep themselves just as busy and active after they have retired by being involved with their community life, or doing voluntary work, many of them for organizations like Help the Aged. Even an interesting hobby can be just as good for helping you feel young.

When I was wondering if I could get back to work, I'd had every thought and consideration in the world given to me by Alan Bell, the Director of *Last of the Summer Wine*. I had my operation in April and was due to be rehearsing for the new series in June, and I had one fear – Alan's such a considerate, good man, and I thought if ever he said to me, 'Thora, could you just . . .?' and if I had to say to him, 'I cannot do that, Alan', I would be broken-hearted. So I thought it was better to be very brave, and say that I couldn't do the next series. And it took a lot for me to say that, because it is such a happy programme to work on. It's been running for ever, and it probably will go on running for ever. There's nothing suggestive in it, and young and old can and do enjoy it.

Just as I was about to say it, Alan said 'Well, you see, I've seen all ten scripts.' I said, 'Oh yes. And supposing that there's something that you ask me to do and . . .' He held up his hand. 'Hold on! You can drink a cup of coffee, can't you?' I said, 'Yes.' He said, 'Well, you've the coffee morning in all ten. Every one. You can get in the car, can't you?' And I said, 'Well, just between the wheel and the seat . . .' And he said, 'Yes, well you won't have any more problems with that, because we are building a false front. And the car will be on a low loader, so there's no effort getting in. There is nothing in all the ten scripts that a dog or cat couldn't do – well if they were clever!'

So you see, being older hasn't affected me there. Until recently I could walk for a short distance without a stick – with pain – but now I've had my operation, I hope that I shall be walking without a stick and without pain. And even if I do have to use my stick, I'm not going to grumble about that. Plenty of people younger than me use sticks.

I was in the hospital for five weeks, giving everything time to heal. And now I'm home, helping to write this little book, and hoping very much to be at the service at Westminster Abbey, where we are going to sing some of the marvellous hymns that some of you have written for it.

You know, I've always thought that some hymns are for special occasions. Well, we know they are. But hymns are, normally, general hymns. But I can give you one tip, if you want a good one

to weed to – weeding the garden – you want 'What
a friend we have in Jesus' because you've just time
to make the pulls.

'What a friend we have in ...' (one pull, one pull)
'Jesus ...' (one pull, one pull)
'All our pains and grief to bear ...' (one pull, one
    pull)

I don't know what order these hymns you've
written are going to be sung in, but I've put them
together in four little piles. The first pile has
hymns for 'doers', who 'keep on keeping on', like
I've just been talking about, the second pile is all
hymns that are like prayers, the third is for singing
on pilgrimage, and the last pile are all the happy
ones that really sing praises.

When I was little, and I lived in this house next
to the theatre in Cheapside, halfway down the
street was a little bakery, and it belonged to Dora,
so everybody called it Dora's. The teacakes – not
the sort you buy now – were currant or plain, and
they were seven for sixpence. I used to go in for
four currant, three plain, and on a Saturday she
did two bakings, and the second lot came out at six
o'clock, so you had them fairly fresh for Sunday.
Now then, added to the teacakes, the Sally Army
band and singers were always just outside her
shop on a Saturday, so on a Saturday tea-time my
mother would say, 'Go to Dora's, will you, for
sixpenny worth of teacakes, four currant, three
plain ... and don't stand too long singing with the
Salvation Army!' Right. I'd have my teacakes in
my hand – I'd always got 'em first, before they'd

sold out! – and then a little sing. I was only a kid,
and I used to stand there, but nobody said, 'Go
away. You can't stand there.' There was a fisherman, because Morecambe, where I was born, as
you know, is noted for the finest shrimps in the
world! – and Happy Jack was a fisherman, big
fellow, little felt hat, not like felt hats are now, more
that came to a point, and a guernsey, and you
could hear him across at Grange. You never heard
such a voice in your life. You could hear him across
the bay at Barrow-in-Furness when he was
singing! That's how 'Onward Christian Soldiers'
first impressed me, with him singing it, and the
Salvation Army band. And quite honestly, with no
disrespect to Wesleyans, Church of England,
Catholic – or anybody else – nobody sings it as
well as the Salvation Army do! And with the
tambourines – Ohoho! – really great!

But now we've got all these new hymns that
you've written, that are going to be sung in the
service in Westminster Abbey on 1st October, and I
should think in many services like it all over the
country and for many years to come. I'd like to say
how good they are, and how genuine they are.
There is something, I think, about living in a small
place – I'd call Morecambe a small place,
compared with a lot of places – you look forward
to all those little things, they are part of life, and
you do them properly, go to a lot of trouble to get
things right, whether it's bringing up your family,
fishing for shrimps, baking teacakes or singing
hymns with the Sally Army singers and band. I
know you understand this because of the hard
work and sincerity that have gone into these

hymns that you've all written – beautiful! So each and every one of you should be extremely proud of your work. Some of them made me smile – like Wally Horton's 'Three score years and ten' (p. 17) – you read it, he wants a bit longer!

There are four sections to this book, for the four kinds of hymns, for Doers, Prayer hymns, for Pilgrims and Praise hymns, like I've said, and at the end of each of my introductions I've included a few thoughts, prayers or poems for a time of quiet meditation, if you're using this book for a service. If you've read any of my other little *Praise Be* books you will already be familiar with the work of my favourite poet, the great Sister Maud CAH, from All Hallowes, Ditchingham, another person who liked to keep busy right to the end of her days, because she wrote all her poems, which she called 'tail wags', between the ages of 80 and 90. Sadly she has passed away since, but here is one of my favourites, Sister Maud's 'tail wag' number 1:

'Only the tail-end of life is left,' I said,
And into my head
A thought came out of the blue,
A thought from you:
'But that is the cheery end,' you said,
'So see
That you use it for me.'
And I said, 'Amen' and raised my head.
'I will glorify God with a wag', I said!

(*Sister Maud CAH*)

Hymns for Doers

❄

1
God's Servants Bold

Tune: Melcombe

Even to your old age and grey hairs, I
am He who will sustain you.

(*Isaiah 46:4*, NIV)

We praise God's many servants bold
Who served Him well when they were old.
May we be ready for the fight
Though weak our arms or dim our sight.

Moses, at fourscore years, we read,
Was called the Israelites to lead.
Strong in the Spirit did he stand
And led them to the Promised Land.

Though Samuel in advancing years
Of Saul the King was filled with fear,
Relying on God's promise, still
Anointed David at His will.

Old Simeon did not despair –
To see the Christ was all his prayer;
And seeing Mary's holy boy
His heart was filled with heavenly joy.

Of Anna, too, a widow sage
We read in Scripture's holy page.
She saw the Christ, then, heart aflame,
To all the good news did proclaim.

So may we, Lord, both old and young
Your praises sing with tireless tongue,
And trust in Your abundant grace
Until we see You face to face.

Frank Liptrot,
Hitchen, Herts
(*A Lay Reader of 50 years' standing!*)

2
Help for the Aged

Tune: Bunessan

But they that wait upon the Lord shall
renew their strength: they shall mount
up with wings as eagles; they shall run,
and not be weary; and they shall walk,
and not faint.

(Isaiah 40:31, AV)

Help for the aged –
Our Lord's apostles
Appoint anointed
Men for the task.
Follow their footsteps,
Care for our old folk,
Love and respect them
Is all they ask.

Help from the aged –
Value their prayers,
We need their wisdom,
Reading the Word.
We value time spent
Peacefully with them –
Inspired by their faith
We serve our Lord.

Help from the ageless –
Eternal Father.
Missing our loved ones

Yet not alone.
Departing in peace,
Seeing salvation,
Rising like eagles
As we go home.

John Phipps,
Sydney, Gloucestershire

3
Help me be a friend

Tune: Unser Herrscher

A new commandment I give unto you,
that ye love one another; as I have loved
you, that ye also love one another.

(John 13:34, AV)

Let me be Thy hands to others,
Let me share Thy love for me,
Seeing Thee in sisters, brothers,
Simply helping trustingly.
Help me be a friend to others,
As I, Lord, to them show Thee.

Let me share Thy gifts, O Father,
Let me share Thine energy,
Giving out to sister, brother,
Strength and comfort, sympathy.
Help me be a friend to others,
As I, Lord, to them show Thee.

Let me get alongside, Father,
Those who need a friend today.
Lead me to them, Jesus, brother,
Tell me what to do and say.
Help me be Thy friend to others,
Always, only, showing Thee.

Dr Joyce Critchlow,
King Sterndale, Derbyshire

4
Inspire in us

Tune:St Anne

. . . Whatever you did for one of the least
of these brothers of mine, you did for
me.

(Matthew 25:40, NIV)

Inspire in us, O God, to share
In Help the Aged's aim,
That at Your bidding we may care
And help the sick and lame.

We only have one life to use
In service great or small,
To share our skills and not refuse
To listen for Your call.

Our hearts go out to You in love,
Our loving, gentle Lord,
O may You hear our praise above,
By all the earth adored.

With grateful hearts today we come
To thank You, Lord most dear,
For bringing us to praise Your name
In love and worship here.

Dame Joan Bartlett, OBE,

Hammersmith, London

(Hon Director and Founder of Servite Houses)

5
Lord, make us faithful

Tune: Green Pastures

And now abideth faith, hope, charity,
these three; but the greatest of these is
charity.

(1 Corinthians 13:13, AV)

Lord, make me faithful to Your cause,
And strengthen my desire
To fight for justice in Your name,
To fight, and never tire.

Lord, keep us hopeful all our days,
That we may watch and pray.
In times of darkness help us choose
The optimistic way.

Lord give us love that we may see
Your face where there is need.
Grant us Your kindly gentleness,
Expressed in word and deed.

So with the faith and hope and love
Which God alone imparts,
We may be bold to follow Christ
And let Him rule our hearts.

> *Gordon Collins,*
> *Alford, Lincolnshire*

6

Jesus our Lord

Tune: Living Lord

Let your light so shine before men, that
they may see your good works.

(Matthew 5:16, AV)

Jesus, our Lord,
You have given us
Gifts most plenteous,
Thank You, Lord.
Teach us to share our gifts around,
So that in us there may be found
Your love, and may that love expound
Faith in you.

Jesus, our Lord,
Guide us every day,
Both at work and play
By our side.
Let other people see in us
The confidence that makes a must
Our loving others, through a trust
Found in You.

Jesus, our Lord,
You are always true –
Let us work for You
In Your name.
Future uncertain, but we know
Our confidence in You will grow –
Mould us and shape us till we know
All of You.

Jesus, our Lord,
When our day is done,
Problems overcome,
We'll come home.
In everything we aim to do,
May we help others, and win through
Knowing our future's safe with You,
Living Lord.

Norman H Mullis,
Colchester, Essex

7

Threescore Years and Ten

> The days of our years are threescore
> years and ten . . . so teach us to number
> our days: that we may apply our hearts
> unto wisdom.
>
> (*Psalm 90:10, 12*, AV)

Threescore years and ten, that's our allotted span,
Threescore years and ten, that's all we are
   allowed.
Lord, please give me more time, to do the things I
   can
And then I'll come and join You in the end.
Life has been so wonderful, I've lived it to the full,
And now there's still so many things I know I
   ought to do.
Please give me more time that I may do the things
   I can
And then I'll come and join You, and then I'll
   come and join You
And then I'll come and join You in the end.

Life has passed me by much faster than You think.
Now I realize, I'm getting near the brink.
If You give me more time, I'll do the best I can,
And then I'll come and join you in the end.
Life has been so wonderful, there's so much more
   to do
Before I leave this world, I would like to see it
   through.
So please, Lord, give me more time, to do the best

I can
And then I'll come and join You, and then I'll
   come and join You
And then I'll come and join You in the end.

Wally Horton
Canterbury, Kent
(Wally composed this hymn on his 70th birthday,
nearly five years ago.)

8
A Simple Faith

Tune: Sagina

Wait on the Lord; be of good courage.
(*Psalm 27:14, AV*)

For me, I need a simple faith:
To trust and know my Saviour's love,
For calmness when I feel distrait,
The deep, blue calm of heaven above;
Teach me, O Lord, to do Your will,
And my faint heart with courage fill.
Teach me, O Lord, to do Your will,
and my faint heart with courage fill.

So many times my way I lose,
But You, my Saviour, know I try;
Help me the one true way to choose
That I may let all else go by;
Teach me, O Lord, to do Your will,

And my faint heart with courage fill.
Teach me, O Lord, to do Your will,
And my faint heart with courage fill.

Dear Lord, I come to You each day
For strength to cope, for patience too,
Stay with me through the night I pray
When I'm alone and needing you;
Teach me, O Lord, to do Your will,
And my faint heart with courage fill.
Teach me, O Lord, to do Your will,
And my faint heart with courage fill.

Without my faith, where would I be?
For I am selfish, weak and poor.
But You, my Saviour, cherish me
And ask me just to love You more;
Teach me, O Lord, to do Your will,
And my faint heart with courage fill.
Teach me, O Lord, to do Your will,
And my faint heart with courage fill.

Molly Rodgers,
South Molton, Devon

9
Christian endeavour

Tune: Land of Hope and Glory

Love never gives up.

(1 Corinthians 13:7)

We, the older people, need Your loving care –
As we seek to serve You, hear our loving prayer.
With Your help and guidance, we shall battle
    through
All that comes upon us, Your love brings peace,
All that comes upon us, Your love brings peace.

Let us all keep cheerful as the days go by,
Help out one another, comfort those that sigh.
We all need each other, young and old alike.
Father, bless our efforts – Your love brings joy,
Father, bless our efforts – Your love brings joy.

Often trials seem heavy we may have to bear,
But we've felt Your presence round us every-
    where.
So with understanding from our years gone by
We can soothe our young folk – Your love quells
    fear,
We can soothe our young folk – Your love quells
    fear.

Now with thanks, dear Father, we do humbly
    pray,
Receive our hope and yearning to live better day
    by day.
For we want to serve You, tell others of Your love,
Help us not to falter as we worship You,
Help us not to falter as we worship You.

Mrs N C Hall,
Chippenham, Wiltshire

10
When God became our neighbour

Tune: Crüger

Whatever you did for one of the least of
these brothers of mine, you did for me.
(*Matthew 25:40*, NIV)

When God became our neighbour
In coming down to earth,
He took the name of Jesus
From His humble birth.
He always cared for others,
The lonely and the sad;
The helpless and the crippled
In meeting Him, were glad.

He told us that in seeking
For others in their need,
We give to Him devotion
In every loving deed.

So help us to be active
In coming to the aid
Of those who will be feeling
Most worried and afraid.

Release from fear and sadness
The house-bound and the old,
The prisoners of ageing
In our lives enfold;
And may the Lord's compassion
He comes to us to prove,
Bind young and old together
In life-enriching love.

Randle Manwaring
Chichester, West Sussex

11
The Lord's Promise

Tune: St Denio

Even to your old age and grey hairs . . . I
will carry you. I will sustain you and I
will rescue you.

(*Isaiah 46:4*, NIV)

'I'll carry you always', the promise is sure.
God's arm never weakens, His mercies endure,
And Abraham, Moses, and Zachary show
That age plays its part in God's purpose below.

Age carries its wisdom, compassion and love,
A peace and tranquillity none can remove;
But also a frailty, dimness of eye,
Heart failing in strength, legs not now so spry.

'I'll carry you always', says God to His own,
And Jesus has now to His Father returned;
He leaves us to carry, to help, to befriend,
To comfort, to cheer, by the grace He will send.

To be a Samaritan, not 'passing by'
When helpers are wanted to answer a cry,
When neighbours are seen in each person in need,
When Jesus can live in each word and each deed.

'I'll carry you always' – let's not fail the task
In helping our neighbour before we are asked.
For with God's commission we're all given aid
To use every gift in the person He's made.

Dr Joyce Critchlow,
King Sterndale, Derbyshire

2

I live alone, dear Lord

❄

What makes this loneliness and anguish
is not that I have no one to share my
burden, but this, I have only my own
burden to bear.

(*Dag Hammarskjold*)

Litany for the Semi-invalid

From the fear of getting worse
    Good Lord, deliver us;
From self-pity and the temptation to play for
        sympathy
    Good Lord, deliver us;
From the fear that others may think we are
        making a fuss
    Good Lord, deliver us;
From self-conscious pride in fighting bravely
        against illness
    Good Lord, deliver us;
From refusal to accept help kindly offered
    Good Lord, deliver us.
When we are enclosed in trouble, and cannot look
        outwards
    Dear Lord, be with us.

For the time to think, because we cannot escape
   into doing
For the opportunities to really listen to the
   problems of others
For the kindness and wisdom of those who help
   us
For the understanding and skill of doctors and
   nurses
For the work of those researching new medicines
   and ways of healing
   We praise you, Good Lord.

In the name of God the Father, whose strength is
   ever with us
And of God the Son, whose suffering delivered us
And of God the Holy Ghost, whose presence is
   our constant comfort.

Amen.

(*Clemency Greatorex, Goudhurst, Kent*)

Miss Greatorex was one of many kind people who,
over the years when I was presenting hymns on
Praise Be on television, would send me prayers
they had written themselves, for me to share, and
I always found so much wisdom in them. And
some of the hymns included in this book are as
much like prayers as hymns, so I've put all these
'prayer-hymns' together, into this section, so now
you'll know where to find them.

   As you get older, prayer time becomes more and
more precious and important. Sometimes my
prayers at night are so long these days I have to
say to the Lord, 'Please excuse me if I don't finish

before I fall asleep. I don't want to be rude, but I think I had better come back to you in the morning.' And in the morning, I'll carry on where I left off. I may just get as far as swinging my legs over the side, and then I'll think, 'I've still got more prayers to do.' So I don't get up until I've finished.

I wonder how many of you have got a habit that I've got, and I know it's a nuisance – I'm a great hoarder. I look at a saucer. This is true. I look at a saucer that was probably a tea-set my husband bought me when we were courting, and all that's left is a saucer, and I think, 'Oh, well, I can't throw that away. No, I'll put a plant pot on it.' And as a result – a lot of rubbish I've got – rubbish, rubbish, that nobody else would keep!

Last year we moved out of one cottage into another one. So in between, all the stuff was downstairs in our big garage in the mews in London. So Jan said, 'I'll go through it with you, Mummy.' Because she is a great chucker-awayer, do you see. And she'd say, 'You don't want this, do you?' Pyoo – in a black bag it went, for the dust-bin. I said, 'What was it?' 'Well, it was an odd cup. You don't wa . . .' 'Well, let me look, if it was . . .'

And really it was a day of, 'Hold on a minute, Jan, let me see, let me see . . .' and so much stuff was got rid of, that now while I'm telling you I've forgotten what it was, so it can't have been that valuable! She'll go through my clothes cupboard. 'Mummy, you don't want this, do you?' 'Well, I might like . . .'

'You don't *want* it, darling. Send it to Oxfam. Let me get a lot of stuff for Oxfam. Let me have stuff for this and that . . .' and she gets my stuff cleared out. She will come in, and look at my desk. Now I must admit – my desk – I sometimes don't know whether to declare it open or set fire to it! There's fan mail, there's letters asking me to open this and open that. And she'll say, 'Have you gone through that pile?' 'No.' 'Right' and she'll go through it, and I'll see her throwing stuff away. She'll say, 'Well, it's just stuff. You don't want to know about somebody who comes cleaning – or who are the best carpet cleaners round Bayswater? No, this is rubbish! You don't want this.'

I wish I could be like that, but I bet there's a lot of you reading this who are like me and keep stuff, don't you? I look in my drawers sometimes and I'll think, 'Oh! I'll have a real chuck out here!' And I find by the time the drawer goes back there's as much stuff in it as when I took it out, and all I've done is revive a lot of memories. But that's how I am, you see. I've always had very vivid memories of my childhood, because it was such a happy one. So I've always thought about it and remembered things that happened, it's not just something I've started to do since I got older. But it is one of the nicest ways to spend your time as you do get older, especially if you have to be sitting still longer than you'd like.

I had a brother, Neville, God rest him. Best brother in the world. There was only a year and nine months between us. My mother used to sing hymns to him to get him to sleep, and my father used to sing comic songs to me, to get me to sleep, and my mother said, 'It was very different, if ever I was trying to get you to sleep, and I sang a comic song. You weren't having that. You'd have it with your father singing it, but not me.' And Neville was the one who would always want hymns. It's strange, isn't it? You'd think I'd have wanted hymns.

Loneliness is the hardest part, for many people, of growing old. Especially when your life-long partner dies and your children have all grown up and gone away, as so many do. I know when I was working on *Praise Be* I used to get so many letters from people who said they didn't have a soul to talk to from the beginning of the week to the end. And that was one of the reasons I liked doing the programmes, because I felt that I could help, even if it was only a little, by being like a friend coming into their living room on a Sunday evening. I hate to think of anyone being so lonely.

Somebody said to me, 'You do a lot, don't you, Thora, for Help the Aged and Age Concern?' And I said, 'Well, I'm one of them, aren't I?' I'm 84 now – I've had another birthday since my operation. Well, I know that's not *that* old, especially when I looked at the Queen Mother last May, standing outside Buckingham Palace, 94, who joined in all the words, did you notice? with the songs on VE Day? Wonderful! And all I worried about was – I wish somebody would come out and give her a chair!

I did a radio broadcast from my hospital bed in May – it was Help the Aged, Age Concern, Carers National Association, Charities Aid Foundation and the Women's Royal Voluntary Service – five organizations who had joined together to form another (Action for Age) – not to finish their own – but to form another thing, which is because, as I said in the broadcast, so many of us pensioners don't realize the benefits there are, if you go about them. I'd promised to do the broadcast before I went into hospital, and the producer, Sandy – that's Judith Chalmers' sister – said to me, 'Well, you won't be able to do it now, will you?' and I said, 'Yes, I will! It'll be even better!' So the BBC brought along all their stuff, and I did it from my bed!

Not all young people are the same – it's obvious – some are sporty, some are party-goers, some are shy, some are very hard-working, some are lazy and rude, and some you simply despair of. And not all of us grow old in the same way either, or feel about it in the same way. I suppose my own way is simply to say, 'No, I don't feel old today.' I've never felt old, really, never thought, 'Ah, you poor old thing!' I always think how blessed I am to feel as well as I do, as old as I am. And if you're like me, it does help a lot if, when you get yourself ready to go out in the morning, whether it be to work or for shopping, or just to be about the house, if you think 'No! I don't *feel* any older since yesterday!'

Then again, someone else in their eighties may look on their old age as a very happy time, a golden time, when perhaps for the first time in their busy lives they find they have time to stop and think, and they can be someone who has time for others. And then there's others who really like to wear purple slippers and let rip! So we're not all the same.

Take Age Concern – I hope I'm allowed to mention them, am I? They have an annual Thé

Dansant at Kensington Town Hall, and everyone comes with their bed slippers to dance! I remember going there one year, the Mayor and Mayoress of Kensington, about a couple of thousand old folk from all walks of life, police band playing 'In the Mood'! And the girl sitting next to me was very ... well, interesting – good tweed suit, non-stop smoking – and it was the girl that *Prime Suspect* is written about! The policewoman detective.

There was an old lady on the dance floor – this is perfectly true – 'In the Mood' she's got the bed slippers on, with turned-over tops and a pom-pom on – *twirdle-der, twirdle-der* – on her own – *twirdle-de, twirdle de* – white hair, ever so thin, all her little pink scalp showing through – and this policewoman detective said, 'Oh, look at that poor old soul! I'll put my fag out and go and dance with her.' I said, 'Hold on! Have a care! Do you know many old people?' She said, 'No' and I said, 'Well, I know 'em!' She said, 'Ah no! I can't watch her dancing on her own.' So I said 'Go on then.' So I watched. She put the fag out, went onto the floor and said to the old lady, 'Do you want to dance, love?' And she said, 'Gerr'off! Whey up! I'm enjoying this!' She was laughing all the way back, and she said, 'You were right!'

We're going to have some of your beautiful hymns now. I must mention Mrs Molly Rodgers from South Molton in Devon here, because she sent in so many of her own prayer-hymns and they all are really lovely, and although there were too many for us to include them all, I should think you should do a book of your own, Mrs Rodgers! Just before we come to the hymns, here are some other people's thoughts and prayers that may be helpful in quiet times of meditation and prayer.

> Everything has its wonders, even darkness and silence, and I learn, whatever state I may be in, therein to be content.
>
> *Helen Keller*

> From quiet homes and first beginning,
> Out to the undiscovered ends,
> There's nothing worth the wear of winning,
> But laughter and the love of friends.
>
> *Hilaire Belloc:* Dedicatory Ode

> This only do I ask of Thy extreme kindness,
> That Thou convert me wholly to Thee,
> And Thou allow nothing to prevent me
> from wending my way to Thee.
>
> *St Augustine of Hippo*

Hymns of Prayer

1
When I am old

Tune: Old 124th

When I am old and greyheaded, O God,
forsake me not.

(Psalm 71:18, AV)

When I am old, be with me still, dear Lord,
Give me a friend to share my joy and pain.
Give me Thy Word, to keep me in Thy will,
A hearth to warm, a shelter from the rain,
Food for my need, against the winter's chill.

And help me to be a friend to others, Lord,
To those who have no family, no kin,
Those who are house-bound, longing to be free,
Those who have fears without, or doubts within,
Or who are waiting still to learn of Thee.

Let me be eyes to help the blind, dear Lord,
Ears to the deaf, feet to the lame and weak.
Teach me to share Thy love, that others know
It's not my strength, Lord, nor my will I seek
But Thine, and it's Thy love alone I show.

Then will my life be blest, and theirs, dear Lord,
Old friends united, and new friendships made.
'Thy will be done, Thy kingdom come,' I pray
Not just in heaven, but on earth, indeed:
'Thy will be done, Thy kingdom come' today.

Dr Joyce Critchlow,
King Sterndale, Derbyshire

2
Prayerful harmony

Tune: Now is the hour

When the even was come, they brought
unto Him many that were possessed
with devils: and He cast out the spirits
with His word, and healed all that were
sick.

(*Matthew 8:16*, AV)

This is the hour of prayerful harmony,
Drawing us close to God's divinity,
Knowing His love – we truly then can share –
In His most blessèd Son,
To hear our prayer.

Call on His name, most precious name of all,
He is our Saviour, gracious Lord of all,
He'll comfort you when earthly cares oppress,
Bringing His peace and grace
To richly bless,

His blessèd name brings joy beyond compare,
His arm outstretched will safely hold you there.
Take of His love, so freely given for you;
Daily these precious gifts
Are ever new.

Walk in His love, He offers it today,
So will the future be the King's highway,
Walking with Him to heights as yet unknown;
He'll bring us safely through
And lead us home.

D E Clarke,
Heanor, Derbyshire

3

Ask what you need of God

Tune: Franconia

Ask and you will receive; seek and you
will find; knock and the door will be
opened to you.

(Matthew 7:7)

Ask what you need of God
And He will hear your prayer –
He knows the need within your heart
And what is hidden there.

Come to Him when you seek
And He will show the way.
He knows that you are lost and weak,
Ask for His help each day.

And as you knock, He hears,
He'll open wide the door,
His love will smooth away your fears
And bless you evermore.

Molly Rodgers,
South Molton, Devon

4
My Little Flock

Tune: St Fulbert

Do not be afraid, little flock.

(Luke 12:32)

'My little flock, be not afraid.'
Thus spoke our Saviour dear.
'You have no need to be dismayed
For I am always near.

'My little flock, you need not fear
For I will show the way.
The Kingdom of the Lord is near
If you keep watch and pray.

My little flock, keep close to me,
My kingdom will I give
To all who truly follow me.
Stay close to me – and live.'

Molly Rodgers,
South Molton, Devon

5
Trust and Thanksgiving

Tunes: Duke Street, Galilee or Truro

Trust in God at all times.

(Psalm 62:8)

You are my God, I trust in You,
Your love surrounds me every day,
You show me all that I should do,
And guide me when I go astray.

To You, dear Lord, I bring my dreams,
My hopes, my fears, and all my cares.
Life often is not what it seems –
I need You always to be there.

And now I thank You for Your love,
I thank You for the light You bring,
I dare to raise my eyes above
And look for You, my God and King.

Molly Rodgers,
South Molton, Devon

6
Heavenly Father, Great Creator

Tune: Hyfrydol

I cannot understand, comprehend, analyse or begin to assess adequately the Trinity. I *can* and *do* feel its presence, guidance and influence.

(*Brian Morris, Whitchurch, Shropshire*)

Heavenly Father, great Creator, Lord of all the
　earth and sea,
Hear us as we come before You, in Your might and
　majesty;
Meet us, Father, in Your mercy, help us now to
　know Your love,
Fill our hearts, Lord, with Your Spirit, make us fit
　for life above.

Saviour Christ, we hear Your message from the
　cross of our great shame,
Teach us how to bear the burden and the joys of
　Your sweet name;
Show us, Jesus, how to witness, how to show Your
　grace to men,
That this world of many nations knows the Risen
　Lord again.

Holy Spirit, wise enabler, power of God supreme
　in men,
Gracious Comforter, live in us till our souls are
　whole again;

Be our light in times of darkness, help us, Lord, to
　　feel You near,
True companion, friend within us, life with You is
　　free from fear.

Father, Son and Holy Spirit, one-in-three and
　　three-in-one,
Triune God, we pledge allegiance till Your mighty
　　work is done;
Till Your love is known by all men, and Your will
　　is man's own choice,
And the angel choirs of heaven 'Glory!' sing in
　　mighty voice.

O G Burchill,
Pewsey, Wiltshire

7

O God of love, Thy people bless

Tune: Martyrdom

When God created human beings, He
made them like Himself . . . He blessed
them and named them 'mankind'.

(Genesis 5:2)

O God of love, Thy people bless
The babe, the youth, the old,
Bring all the nations of the earth
Together in Thy fold.

God, bless the Help the Aged cause,
At home and overseas,
Give us the heart, the strength, the means
To join in willingly.

O bless the aged through their years,
Thought give them for the young,
To share their troubles, show them truth,
And heed not race nor tongue.

O bless young people, wisdom grant
That they may understand
The aches and pains and woes of age,
And give a helping hand.

O bless the nations, young and old,
Show them Thy power divine
Then tell them on Thy reaping day,
'Behold, you all are mine!'

BFS

*(BFS is a member of the Women's Fellowship
at Christ Church, Roxeth Hill. She was 94
when she wrote these words.
They 'just came' to her.)*

8
Dear Lord, please help the aged

Tune: Wir Pflügen

Eli realized that it was the Lord who was
calling the boy.

(1 Samuel 3:8)

Dear Lord, please help the aged –
They need your love and care;
Sometimes they find their troubles
Are more than they can bear.
Protect them ere they stumble,
Give comfort when they weep,
Walk with them through the day-time
And guard them when they sleep.

Thank You, God, for listening to what we had to
    say,
We thank You for Your blessings,
As we kneel here and pray.

When asking for Your guidance,
Those in their twilight years
Are certain You can hear them
And understand their fears.
Please grant us peace of mind, Lord,
While we wait for Your call,
As light and life grow dim, Lord,
We need You most of all.

Thank You, God, for listening to what we had to
    say,
We thank You for Your blessings
As we kneel here and pray.

> *Thurza Blurton,*
> *Orpington, Kent*

9
You are God

Tune: O my love

I talked about things I did not understand, about marvels too great for me to
know.

(Job 42:3)

You are God –
Some have doubts of who You are.
You are God –
Some have strayed from You so far.
You are God,
But Your blessèd word will show
A life that's given for us below.
You will speak and we shall know
You are God.

You are God –
All our doubts will disappear.
You are God –
We will pray that You'll be near.

You are God,
So dark days we need not fear,
For You came our sins to bear.
We will listen and will hear:
You are God.

Mary Hudson,
Helensburgh, Dumbartonshire

10
I sought the Lord

Tune: Mundays

He was still a long way from home
when his father saw him; his heart was
filled with pity and he ran, threw his
arms round his son, and kissed him.

(Luke 15:20)

I sought the Lord, and afterwards I knew
He moved my soul to seek Him, seeking me.
It was not I that found Thee, Saviour true,
No, I was found of Thee.

Thou didst reach forth Thy hand and mine
    enfold –
I walked and sank not on the storm-vexed sea.
'Twas not so much that I on Thee took hold
As Thou, dear Lord, on me.

I find, I walk, I love, but Oh, the whole
Of love is but my answer, Lord, to Thee,
For Thou wast long before-hand with my soul,
Always Thou lovest me.

Anon

11
Turn to Jesus

Tune: All for Jesus

Come unto me, all ye that labour and are
heavy laden, and I will give you rest.
(Matthew 11:28, AV)

Are you lonely, are you lonely?
Do you miss somebody dear?
Turn to Jesus, turn to Jesus!
He will evermore be near.

Are you fearful, are you fearful?
What the future may have planned?
Turn to Jesus, turn to Jesus!
Let Him take you by the hand.

Keep on praying, keep on smiling,
Never wear a frown.
Turn to Jesus, turn to Jesus!
He will never let you down.

Greta Ward,
Bracknell, Berks

3

To be a pilgrim

❄

There's no discouragement
Will make him once relent
His first avowed intent
To be a pilgrim.

(*John Bunyan*)

Years may wrinkle the skin, but to give
up enthusiasm wrinkles the soul.

(*Samuel Ullman*)

It does not matter how slow you go,
as long as you do not stop.

(*Confucius*)

I expect many of you are like me and enjoy getting
into the sun for a bit – when and if you can. For the
last two years my holidays have been in the form
of pilgrimages to the Holy Land. Oh beautiful!
Absolutely wonderful. Last year, in May, I cele-
brated my 83rd birthday there, right there – on the
Sea of Galilee – where Jesus had His birthdays, so
you can't do better than that, can you? It was to be
my last birthday with my darling Scottie, but what
better place for him to wish me a last 'Happy
birthday'?

We had arrived at the hotel late the night before,
and as we are both early risers we were both awake
to sit on our balcony and watch the sun rise over the

Sea of Galilee early the next morning. The boats they take you out in look just as they would have in Jesus' time, and even the boatmen were wearing New Testament costume, and you really feel that nothing but time separates you from Jesus and the disciples being there, talking to one another, on the exact same spot. In the middle of the sea the captain turned off the boat's engines, and the sense of tranquillity you get at the moment when the boat is at rest – well, as Scottie said, it can't really be described in words. It was so still, you couldn't even hear water lapping against the side of the boat.

That feeling of being where Jesus had been came over me even more in a place they call the Mount of the Transfiguration, Mount Tabor. This was one of the highlights for me. Of course I couldn't walk up, I went in a taxi, well, we all did, but I could just visualize Jesus with Peter, James and John plodding up this mountain. You can see for miles up there. There's a community of Franciscan friars who have a retreat house at the top, and one of the brothers, Brother Andrew, talked to me and it didn't matter what kind of simple things I asked him, it was as though he'd expected me to ask these things. I said to him: 'Don't think I'm silly, but every time I put my foot to the ground on this mountain, I can't help wondering if Jesus had His foot just there.' And I'll never forget his reply as long as I live. He said, 'If that is where you put your feet, then that is where He put His.'

Cana is not far from Nazareth. I remember thinking, 'I'm glad Mary and Jesus didn't have too far to walk for the wedding feast!' It was about eight minutes by bus. We walked down a little alley to a tiny church. You might know it's the most popular church in the world to get married in! Jimmy and I were married for fifty-eight years, and there in the little church in Cana we renewed our marriage vows together, and I've got a wedding certificate from Cana in Galilee to prove it!

Now I know not everybody can go on pilgrimage, although I would say that if you can possibly go, it's probably the best thing you'll ever do in your life. I used to tell the story on *Praise Be* about the Methodist minister, James Thomas East, who always wanted to visit the Holy Land, and kept meaning to go, but one thing after another kept happening so that he had to see to things at home, and he didn't go. The day came when he realized that he never would go, it was perhaps not God's will for him to go, and that day, feeling very sad and disappointed, he sat down and wrote a lovely little hymn called 'Wise Men Seeking Jesus'. Here are just a few verses:

> Wise men seeking Jesus
> Travelled from afar,
> Guided on their journey
> By a beauteous star.

> But if we desire Him,
> He is close at hand;
> For our native country
> Is our Holy Land.

> Prayerful souls may find Him
> By our quiet lakes,
> Meet Him on our hillsides
> When the morning breaks.

Isn't that beautiful? And it's quite true . . . But I still say – if you can go – go! They say that every actor should do a season at Blackpool, and I say that every Christian should have at least a week in the Holy Land!

After a pilgrimage you see the Bible differently. The stories come to life. The distances between places is much smaller than I'd ever imagined, and everything becomes so real and vivid. Now when I read my Bible or say my prayers my thoughts are often with me from the pilgrimage. And I'm so glad that Jimmy was able to visit the Holy Land before he died.

Some lovely hymns have been written for Help the Aged that I think would be good to sing on a pilgrimage. Once again one person, this time Mary Hudson from Helensburgh, has sent in so many and they are all so good that I've included quite a few. I think you must have visited the Holy Land yourself, Mrs Hudson.

First, here are some thoughts for meditation.

> Sanctify us, O God, pilgrims of the way of Christ, that in this life we may live in purity, humility and love and, at the last, may come to share the glory of your eternal kingdom; through Jesus Christ our Lord. Amen.
>
> *(Part of the prayer used on the Haddington Pilgrimage)*

Every peaceful village
In our land might be
Made by Jesus' presence
Like sweet Bethany.

He is more than near us
If we love Him well;
For He seeketh ever
In our hearts to dwell.

(*James Thomas East*)

The world cannot be discovered by a
journey of miles . . . only by a spiritual
journey . . . by which we arrive at the
ground at our feet, and learn to be at
home.

(*Wendell Berry*)

To keep our faces toward change and
behave like free spirits in the presence of
fate is strength undefeatable.

(*Helen Keller*)

Yesterday's history
Tomorrow's a mystery
Today is a gift –
That is why it is called
The Present!

(*Anon*)

Hymns for Pilgrims

❋

1
To His Glory

Tune: To His Glory

Every valley shall be exalted.

(*Isaiah 40:4*, AV)

Fill the valleys with music,
The hills resound with praise,
Join with us in the glory,
Tell the sacred story.
Sing to all of Lord Jesus,
Your voices loudly raise.

Fill your lives with the Father,
He'll share His love with all,
Join with us in the glory,
Incarnate and holy.
Voices singing to Lord Jesus
Answering unto His call.

Fill your hearts with caring
And journey on your way,
Join with us in the glory,

Bless the One, all holy,
Hail in song the Lord Jesus,
Sing of His glory always.

Mary Hudson,
Helensburgh, Dumbartonshire

2

In my imagination

Tune: Song 1 (Eternal Ruler)

And Peter went out and wept bitterly.
(Luke 22:62)

In my imagination, Lord, I stand
Beside the awful road to Calvary,
But cannot see one member of the band
Who shared the last three vital years with Thee.
Through narrow streets I see Thee with Thy cross
On shoulders weakened by man's cruelty.

And I confess, Lord, I do understand
And know why they have all forsaken Thee.
I follow too, but very far behind,
And see where on the hill Rome's soldiers wait;
I hear the hammer blows, but not one word
Escapes my lips as man pours out his hate.

And as my Lord hangs on that cursèd tree,
A dying thief for love and mercy prays:
He speaks for vile humanity, and me.

For I my Saviour also have betrayed.
I share the fear felt by Thy followers then,
Those who deserted Thee for fear of men.

I follow on, yet still so far behind,
Knowing my great unworthiness of Thee.
And as I watch, within my spirit's mind,
I see Thy face of mercy turn to me.
What can I do but stand outside and weep?
Oh, let me not again crucify Thee.

O G Burchill,
Pewsey, Wiltshire

3
You are our hope

Tune: These are my mountains

We have peace with God through our
Lord Jesus Christ . . . and so we boast of
the hope we have of sharing God's
glory!

(Romans 5:1–2)

You are our hope, Lord,
A bright shining light
To show us the way, Lord,
To know wrong from right.

We go our own way, Lord,
Turn day into night,
But You are our hope, Lord,
And You are our light.

We aren't without hope, Lord,
You gave us Your Son
That good over evil
The fight can be won.

We go our own way, Lord,
Turn day into night
But You are our hope, Lord,
And You are our light.

Mary Hudson,
Helensburgh, Dumbartonshire

4
The road is long and wide

Tune: St Anne

I will not fail thee nor forsake thee. Be
strong and of a good courage.

(Joshua 1:5, 6, AV)

O God, when we are very young
And youth is on our side,
Our minds are all on earthly things,
The road is long and wide.

Life has a way of speeding past,
And we're surprised to find
That all the time we thought we had –
Is nothing of the kind!

When age is bearing down on us
In its relentless way,
We know we need Thy love and care –
We know our need to pray.

And now our time is getting short
And our thoughts turn to home,
Give us that peace of mind we sought,
That's Thine and Thine alone.

And when that great day comes, dear Lord,
When we shall be with Thee,
O God, we shall rejoice and sing
Through all eternity.

Doreen A Mayers,
Huntingdon, Cambridgeshire

5
These Things Happened in Palestine

Tune: Dundee

And behold, a woman in the city, which
was a sinner, when she knew that Jesus
sat at meat in the Pharisee's house,
brought an alabaster box of ointment.

(*Luke 7:37*, AV)

These things happened in Palestine,
Magdaka, now Mejdel,
And in the days of Jesus Christ
Great wealth therein did dwell.

Beside the valley where the doves
Are bred for sacrifice,
There lived a fallen prostitute
Who Christ did not despise.

Then in the house of Simon
A certain Pharisee
Who snubbed Our Lord when he arrived
No greeting kiss gave he.

A shadow followed Jesus in,
A moonbeam in the night.
And Mary, with a grateful heart,
Kept Jesus in her sight.

And when she saw how little love
Was given to Him there
She washed His blessed feet with tears
And dried them with her hair.

Mary Hudson,
Helensburgh, Dumbartonshire

6
The Robe

Tune: Ebenezer (O the deep, deep love of Jesus)

If I just touch His clothes, I will be
healed.

(Mark 5:28, NIV)

Oh to touch the robe of Jesus
And be healed for evermore!
Oh to feel that love divine flow
From His being, into mine!
Lord, as You love me, O let me love You,
Teach me to love the way You do,
Love those that love You, love those that need You,
Love those who need to be healed by You.

Oh to touch the robe of Jesus
And be healed and pure once more!
Like a child, with no more hurting
In my soul for evermore!
Lord, as You love me, O let me love You,
Teach me to love the way You do,
Love those that love You, love those that need You,
Love those who need to be healed by You.

C Flint,
Harrow, Middlesex

7
Somebody knows

A man takes a mustard seed, the smallest seed in the world, and plants it in the ground . . . it grows up and becomes the biggest of all plants.

(*Mark 4:31–2*)

Somebody knows why the green grasses grow,
And He knows why night follows day,
Somebody knows which way we should go,
Someone can show us the way.
  Someone I know made the tiny seeds grow
  Into flowers that blossom through snow.
  I look all around at the treasures I've found
  Since finding this Someone I know.

Somebody hears, when I start to pray,
For the troubles this world can unfold,
Somebody knows and shows me the way,
Somebody makes it less cold.
  Someone I know . . .

Somebody's hand commanded the sea,
Made mountains so rivers could flow,
Somebody knows which way I should go
Now I know, for He told me so.
  Someone I know . . .

J. Ricks

8
Going Home

Tune: Hyfrydol

In my Father's house are many mansions.
(John 14:2, AV)

I am going home to Jesus,
Going to the Promised Land.
He'll be waiting there to greet me,
He'll be there with outstretched hand.
House of Jesus! House of Jesus!
What a welcome there will be!
House of Jesus! House of Jesus!
What a welcome there will be!

All my sins will be forgiven,
I'll be from my bondage free.
In His house a peaceful haven,
He'll be there to cherish me.
Peace of Jesus, peace of Jesus,
Never will I part from Him.
Peace of Jesus, peace of Jesus,
Never will I part from Him.

All my strife and all my trouble
All my mortal toil and fears.
He'll be at the door to greet me,
He'll be there to dry my tears.
Love of Jesus! Love of Jesus!
All-enfolding love He'll give.
Love of Jesus! Love of Jesus!
All-enfolding love He'll give.

Mary Hudson,
Helensburgh, Dumbartonshire

9

Most Blessèd Mary

Tune: Winchester New

And the angel said unto her, 'Fear not,
Mary: for thou hast found favour with
God.'

(Luke 1:30, AV)

Most blessèd Mary, chosen one
To be the Mother of God's Son,
By wonders of the holy birth
God's love came down from heaven to earth.

Mother Jesus, joy bells rang
And angel hosts from heaven sang.
'Magnificat' was Mary's praise,
We share her joy, now and always.

We honour God's most blessèd one,
Who gave her all for her dear Son,
Till joy turned into tears and grief,
But steadfast stayed in her belief.

We can but partly visualize
The dreadful scene that met her eyes,
But from that death on cross of pain
Came life restored, and hope again.

We plead that Mary's faith and love
Will bring us blessings from above,
To give us faith along life's way
And strength to do God's will each day.

'Thy kingdom come, Thy will be done!'
We worship God, and His dear Son.
We join praise with the saints in light
And dear ones passed beyond our sight.

We journey onwards hopefully,
With faith and trust that all will be
Revealed in glory, and we pray
That we're found worthy on that day.
                                    Amen.
                          G V Goodchild,
                          Sandy, Bedfordshire

10
By Galilee

Tune: St Cuthbert (Our blessed redeemer)

'Didn't you know that I had to be in my
Father's house?' . . . Jesus went back
with them to Nazareth, where He was
obedient to them.

> (*Luke 2:49, 51*)

Along the shores of Galilee,
By roads of Nazareth,
Along the cobbled streets walked He
Of all men blessed.

The camels trod their ancient route,
And Jesus saw them pass.
The merchants from the East and West
Great wealth amassed.

But He had greater work by far,
Blessed by His Father's call.
No gold for Him, but healing love
To save us all.

Mary Hudson
Helensburgh, Dumbartonshire

11
In Waltham Abbey, Essex

Tune: Calypso Carol

She . . . laid Him in a manger.

(*Luke 2:7*)

Here is warmth and light and christmassing,
And here is music to the rafter borne.
Here's the magic of a baby born
To all mankind, in cold grey dawn.
  In our church, we are at Bethlehem.
  Here's the crib where Christ appeared to men,
  A tree, and little Mary, full of grace,
  There's candlelight on every face.

Trees outside are bright with garlands red,
The grass is cold with spears of frost abroad.
Carol singers in the windy market-place
Remind us all that Christ is Lord.
  In our church . . .

And in our church, upon the altar bare
Still stands a cross, in all the light around –
For God at Christmas time is showing all His love:
Humility with glory crowned.
  In our church . . .

                    Mr and Mrs Killick,
                    Barnet, Hertfordshire

4

Salute to Scottie

❄

One inch of joy surmounts of grief a span,
Because to laugh is proper to the man.

(Francois Rabelais)

All shall be Amen and Alleluia.
We shall rest and we shall see,
We shall see and we shall know,
We shall know and we shall love,
We shall love and we shall praise.
Behold our end which is no end.

(St Augustine of Hippo)

It's a funny thing to say to people in a book, is this.
Well not funny – I don't mean FUNNY. I mean
strange: I didn't know what a stroke was. At least, I
knew what a stroke *was*, but what I mean to say is,
I wouldn't know if I'd seen anybody have a stroke.

I was combing my hair in my room one morning
– and it's quite a small mews house we live in in
London – and Scottie had gone through into the
bathroom to shave. And while I was combing my
hair I heard a crash on the floor, like one of my big
copper pans falling off the wall. And I called out,
'Is that one of the pans that's fallen off the wall?'
But he didn't answer, so I just put my comb down,
and I went to look in the kitchen. But there was no
pan on the floor. I saw the light on in the bathroom,

and I went in and there was Scottie, fallen backwards into the bath, as if in a faint. But his legs were over the side of the bath from the knees. Do you follow what I mean? His knees and feet. And it sounds such a terrible thing to say, but it's true, and I loved him and I thought, 'Oh, doesn't he always have such clean shoes?' They were so polished, you know, his shoes. And at the same time I said to him, 'What is it, darling? Did you go dizzy or something?' And he didn't answer me, but he sort of put one arm out a little bit, so I got hold of it, realizing that from the position he was in there was no way I could pull him out. There was no water in the bath or anything, but he had broken the tray that had all the sponges and soap, and it's a wonder it hadn't cut his neck open, but he was spared that.

I ran to the telephone. I'm blessed with good neighbours, and I said to Gail, who is a dear friend of mine, 'Gail, Scottie has slipped and fallen. Is Bob there?' Because I knew her husband was a big strong fellow. And she said 'Oh, Thora, he's out, but hold on . . .' and she hung up. So I went back into the bathroom, and Jimmy was still there, not saying anything. As a matter of fact he never said anything again. Ever. But at that point I wasn't aware of that. And suddenly Gail rushes in with a gentleman I've never seen in my life before – well, nobody in the mews had, he'd just bought a mews house the week before – and as she came out of the door, she's an American, she'd said, 'Hey, neighbour, we're needed. Come on!' So he followed her! Well, none of us could move Jimmy, and she said, 'I've rung for an ambulance.'

I have to give the ambulance service full marks – they were no time at all. And two ambulance men came upstairs, and one said, 'Go downstairs, Thora. Or in the other room. We know exactly how to pick your husband up.' Which they did, and took him down, and Gail and I went to the hospital with him.

What I want to say is – I'm not being a clever dick with any of you – but you can write to the Stroke Association in London and get a booklet, telling all you need to know about strokes. There are more people than you'd ever realize die *in a day* in the world, with a stroke. And this was a massive stroke from which Scottie never recovered. And after three weeks, they made a hole in his stomach and put a tube in to try and feed him, or shall I say, try to keep him alive. But he didn't know us or anything. And I came home that Saturday, after they'd put the tube in, at tea-time. I never wanted to leave him if I thought he was awake, but I don't think he ever really knew any of us. No, that's wrong. My granddaughter flew over from America, and my grandson, and she was so upset because she loved him so dearly. She said, 'Poppa? It's Daisy . . . Squeeze my hand if you know it's me.' And he squeezed her hand. So he must have known that one.

But we always sat with him, Jan and I. And I never liked to leave him in case he was awake, and yet I knew he wasn't awake. And when I got home that Saturday, I went into my bedroom and I sat very quietly on my bed and I said, 'Please, God, here I am again, asking another favour. Would you take Scottie, in his sleep?'

Well, that was seven o'clock. At two in the morning my telephone rang in my room. Jan was staying in the next room and the telephone rang there too, so she answered it, and she came in and she said, 'Mummy . . . Daddy's free.'

I don't want you to think that because I asked for him to die, God took him. I am quite convinced, very convinced, that God would have taken him whether I'd said that or not. Because I think God knows when he wants you to go. But it just happened to coincide that it happened after I'd said, 'Please take him in his sleep,' and it's just that I'm so grateful. I know it sounds funny to say.

And when we went to the hospital, as we did then, at two in the morning, with dear John Tudor, our minister, coming in from the country, and I don't know how he got there as soon as we did, Scottie was on his side, just as I'd left him that tea-time, *just* as I'd left him, and I thought, 'Thank you, God.' And I mean, for a woman who loved her husband as much as I loved mine – but I didn't cry. I just looked at him, lying there so peacefully just as though he were asleep.

I've pictures round of him laughing at me. Really laughing – he'd a good laugh. And believe you me, he's with me *so much*. I don't mean I can see him or feel him or anything. I just know he's there. And while I was in the hospital myself recently, when they said, 'We're just going to give you a couple of pills now, before we take you into the operating theatre.' I whispered to Scottie 'Be with me.' And I know he was. Because I'm here, writing this, aren't I?

A few weeks later I went with Jan on another

pilgrimage. We'd arranged it long before and
Scottie should have come with us. It was to Jordan
and Petra this time. Beautiful. And one day we
were standing on a sort of cliff edge, looking far
out to where we could see Galilee, and on this
ledge was a little church, and it was like wattle and
daub, like those very old cottages, and inside there
weren't any pews. There were long forms, with
sort of leather tops. No backs. And as I went in, I
said to Jan, 'This is the sort of church your Daddy
would have said, "Now this is a *real* church."'
There was nothing, really, about it at all, only, I
don't know, a feeling of love in it. And I sat down
and I – like most of us who've lost the ones we love
– well, often – one doesn't cry until a few weeks
after. I didn't with my mother, I know. And I
suddenly thought, 'Oh, I'm going to cry.' And I
said to Jan, 'I'm going to cry.' And she said, 'Well
cry, Mummy,' and put her arms round my shoulders.

When I was doing the programme *Praise Be*,
which I did for seventeen years, I got so many sad
letters, and I really mean heart-breaking, some of
them were, and I'd read them, and be upset. I
always say in my prayers, 'Please, God, comfort
the grief-stricken.' Because grief is the most
terrible pain.

I haven't felt that kind of pain about Scottie. I've
been spared that. I think it's because, to me, he's
still here. I say good morning to his picture every
morning, and goodnight, God bless, every day.
But I don't really understand it as far as the crying
goes. Because nobody could love their husband
more than I loved him.

But anyway, when I was crying over these *Praise Be* letters, Scottie would come in the room and he would say, 'Now, come on.' That's three words: Now, come, on – which meant – 'we don't want any crying.'

And I sat on this form in this little wattle-and-daub church, and I felt the tears starting at the base of my stomach and coming up – the heartbreak I felt in my body – and just about a foot in front of me, I don't mean I saw anything, there was nothing to see, but as clearly as I'm saying this to you, I heard him say, 'Now, come on.' And I stopped. I didn't cry.

Jan said to me afterwards, when we got outside, 'Maybe a good cry would have done you good.' I said, 'No, your father told me not to.'

At the funeral, taken by our dear friend John Tudor at Westminster Central Hall chapel, we had his favourite hymn, 'Oh Happy Day', and some jazz music that he used to play when he was a drummer with the band, and different people, friends, and Daisy and James, all stood up in turn and said how great he'd been and different things about him, and it sounds funny to say this, but it really was a joyous occasion, and at the end Jan shouted out, 'Well done, Dad!'

The night before the organist had telephoned me and he said, 'Is this the tune?' and he played it. I said 'No! No! Oh – No!' And there was Jan and me, each on a different telephone extension going, 'O happy day, O happy day when Jesus washed my sin away . . .' and, 'OK, I've got that', he says, so he played it, and we carried on: 'He taught me how to watch and pray, and grow more loving every day . . .' – we got to about there, and he said, 'All right, I've got it now.' But the following day he told me, 'I don't know. I'm that nervous', and to be honest, it didn't go quite right. Jan managed to keep going, but there seemed to be more words than tune, if you know what I mean, so most of us kept getting lost. Which was a shame, but there you are.

We've got Scottie's ashes, and John Tudor came down to the cottage, because we've got two rose-beds 48 feet long each, from the front door to the gate, and he put them on there, and said a little prayer. It was there because we sat having a cup of coffee outside last summer, and Jimmy had said, 'Aren't those roses beautiful?' And I said, 'Aren't they lovely!' and he said, 'And aren't we bluddy lucky to have all this?' That's what he said! And afterwards I thought, 'That's the place.'

Well, I don't know if any of this last lot of hymns can be sung to the tunes of 'Onward Christian Soldiers' or 'O Happy Day', the two hymns I want at my own funeral – I leave that to some clever head who knows about tunes – but I do know that they are all *great*, really good praise hymns, and I hope we'll be singing some of them together in October. Before I finish, let me leave you with two more thoughts for your meditations.

> With every person who dies, part of us is already in eternity. We must, if we love this person, live up to the great en-counter of a living soul with a living God. We must let go of everything that

was small, that was separation, alien-
ation and estrangement, and reach out
to that serenity and greatness, newness
and abundance of life into which the
departed person has entered. We should
not speak of our love in the past tense.
Love is a thing that does not fade in a
faithful heart. It does not go into the past
unless we betray our love. We must
keep our love alive in a new situation,
but as actively and creatively, and more
so, more often, than when the person
was with us. Our love cannot be dead
because a person has died. If that is true,
our life must be a continuation of theirs,
with all its significance. We must reflect
on all that was beauty, and nobility in
that person, and make sure those
around us, and our surroundings, do
not lose anything through the death.
This applies to all families and friends as
well as the immediate bereaved, so that
the seed that has fallen into corruption
may give a hundredfold harvest in the
hearts and lives of others.

(*Metropolitan Anthony of Sourozh*)

God's in his heaven –
All's right with the world!

(*Robert Browning:* Pippa Passes)

Songs of Praise

1
Sing Praises

Tune: Repton

Let everything that hath breath praise
the Lord!

(*Psalm 150*, AV)

O God, although our youth has flown,
The flame burns brightly still.
Through years of change, through storm and
    strife
Now in the autumn of our life,
We sing our praise to Thee,
We sing our praise to Thee.

The plans we've made may go awry,
Our dreams and hopes all fade,
But love of family, love of friends,
Eternal love that never ends,
Help us along the way,
Help us along the way.

Amidst the turmoil all around,
May we retain our pride.
The golden rule we should apply,

To do as we would be done by,
That makes a kinder world,
That makes a kinder world.

However long the night may seem,
As grief and pain increase,
To feel Thy presence very near
Will comfort and allay our fear,
And give us inner peace,
And give us inner peace.

S Leheup
Sidcup, Kent

2
This is the Day

Tune: Londonderry Air

I have been with you wherever you
have gone.

(*2 Samuel 7:9*)

This is the day the Lord our God has brought to
   us,
This is the day when all life springs to view,
This is the day that all that He has wrought in us
We bring to Him, to dedicate anew.
We bring our praise, our thanks, our adoration,
We bring our love, the favours of our day.
We lay them on Your altar, our oblation,
We sanctify them with our love and praise.

This is the way the Lord has led us lovingly,
This is the way He wills for us to tread,
This is the way we go in love, confidingly –
The way to Him so sure, so clear ahead.
With Him we go, knowing His hand is over us,
We thank Him for the guidance that we know.
O Father God, because of all You've given us,
We trust You for the way that we have still to go.

Elizabeth Killick,

High Barnet, Hertfordshire

3

Hail to Thee, Almighty King

Tune: Skye Boat Song

This God – how perfect are His deeds!
... He is like a shield for all who seek His
protection.

(Psalm 18:30)

Almighty God, omnipotent One,
We adore Thee.
Each new day enfolded in love,
Our thanks we give to Thee.

Hail to Thee,
Almighty King,
To Thee our praise we sing.
Hail to Thee,
Almighty King,
To Thee our praise we bring.

Shall we despair, who know Thy love?
All those who trust in Thee,
Thou giv'st us strength to carry on,
All through eternity.

Hail to Thee,
Almighty King,
To Thee our praise we sing.
Hail to Thee,
Almighty King,
To Thee our praise we bring.

Father and Lord, who art in heaven,
Hallowed be Thy name.
Thy kingdom, Thy will be done,
In earth and heaven the same.

Amy Levy
London N17

4
Praise

Tunes: School House or Welwyn
(O Strength and Stay)

God is our refuge and our strength . . .
(Psalm 46:1, AV)

Almighty God, my strength against temptation,
My guide, my help to follow in Your ways,
My Lord and God, my source of inspiration,
To You I bring my offering of praise.

Lord God of hosts, ruler of every nation,
While praises to Your glory rise above,
To You I bring in humble adoration
The gifts You gave me, Lord, to use with love.

Dear Lord of heaven and King of all creation
From mountains high, to seas of depths unknown,
Giver of life and all that brings salvation,
I come to worship now before Your throne.

Molly Rodgers
South Molton, Devon

5
Harvest Praise

Tune: Open my eyes

A grain of wheat remains no more than a
single grain unless it is dropped into the
ground and dies. If it does die, then it
produces many grains.

(John 12:24)

The autumn leaves fall to the ground,
There in the soil they will be found,
They are not useless, blown away –
They feed the soil for each new day.
The wheat and corn are gathered in,
Wonder that dead seed lives again.
Praise to God's name! All glory be!
Sing happily.

Thanks for maturity of mind,
For the machinery of mankind,
The harvester, the tractor, plough,
Lessening the work and sweat of brow.
Thanks for the milk and sugar beet,
Praise to our Lord for all we eat,
Praise for the gifts that God gives us –
So wondrous.

Do not forget, God loves each one,
He sent to earth His only Son.
Full fruitful life our Saviour led
Then crucified, for us He bled,
But lives again, and brings us peace
Through which the pains of sin will cease.
And when God's harvest comes at last,
Our sorrows pass.

                                                (Anon)

Sing With Praise

6
God the Father

Firmly I believe and truly
God is three and God is one.
(*John Henry Newman*)

God the Father, throned in glory,
Ageless Lord of time and space,
Worlds-creating, life-sustaining,
Laws disclosed in nature's face:
Shared throughout the human race.

God the Son, in whom compassion,
Healing, saving grace abound,
Faith inspiring, persevering,
Crucified on Calvary's mound:
Risen Lord, ascended Victor,
Christ in glorious triumph crowned.

God the Spirit, source of power,
Shown in tongues and wind and flame,
Fill with faith, hope, love and wisdom
All who call upon Thy name,
Truth with justice, peace and wholeness
May Thy people's life proclaim.

Father, Son and Holy Spirit,
Honour, praise, dominion be!
Help the aged, guide the carers,
Grant the dead to rest in Thee.
Help us all to help each other,
Bless us, Holy Trinity.

Ruth Dunston,
Exeter, Devon

7
Eternal Day

Tune: Stuttgart or Shipston

We know that in all things, God works
for good with those who love Him,
those whom He has called according to
His purpose.

(Romans 8:28)

We were born, and through our childhood
Parents gave us love and care;
As we grew in strength and stature,
God, unseen, was everywhere.

Through our youth and years which followed,
Even when we paid no heed,
He was there in times of danger –
His sure hand filled every need.

Now as eventide draws nearer,
Thanks and praise to God ascend,
For our memories so precious,
And the hope that knows no end.

Father, who creates and guides us,
All Your mercies we survey.
May Your presence still be near us
Who enter Your eternal day.

Gordon R Collins,
Alford, Lincolnshire

8

O What a Joy to have Jesus

Tune: How Great Thou Art

The surpassing worth of knowing Jesus
Christ my Lord . . .

(Philippians 3:8, RSV)

At work, at home, with friends or quite alone,
O what a joy to know Christ Jesus!
To feel His presence and His wondrous love,
So freely given to all the universe.
O what a joy to know Christ Jesus!
O what a joy, such a great joy,
O what a joy to love Christ Jesus!
O what a joy! O what a joy!

When others laugh at us, so cruelly mocking,
O what a joy to know Christ Jesus!
His faithfulness is like a mighty fortress –
He lived and died and rose again for us.
O what a joy to know Christ Jesus!
O what a joy, such a great joy,
O what a joy to love Christ Jesus!
O what a joy! O what a joy!

So walk with God, be tall and strong and straight,
O what a joy to know Christ Jesus!
Give Him your love, your hope and all your faith,
And one day you'll see His belovèd face.
O what a joy to know Christ Jesus!
O what a joy, such a great joy,
O what a joy to love Christ Jesus!
O what a joy! O what a joy!

Olwen M Porter,
Poole, Dorset

(Olwen tells us how this hymn was written over fifty years
ago in Newport, Gwent, for Whitsun. It appeared in a
special hymn sheet with five other hymns for 6d [2½p today].
Since losing her husband, Olwen lives in sheltered
accommodation in Poole, and regularly attends her local
Methodist church.)

9
Now as we grow old, Lord

Tune: Eudoxia

I will not leave you comfortless, I will come to you.

(*John 14:18*, AV)

Now as we grow old, Lord,
Keep us in Thy care.
May Thy loving presence
Be forever there.

Guide us by Thy wisdom,
When to Thee we call.
Help us when we stumble,
Lift us when we fall.

When in times of sadness,
Comfort and sustain,
Calm the troubled spirit,
Ease the body's pain.

Now as we grow old, Lord,
May we surely find
Strength for each tomorrow,
Hope for all mankind.

Joan Barson,
Farnborough, Hampshire

10
Russell

Tune: The Lincolnshire Poacher

God has shown us how much He loves
us – it was while we were still sinners
that Christ died for us.

(Romans 5:8)

We thank You, Lord, for all Your love toward the
    sons of men,
We thank You for Your promise that Your son will
    come again,
We thank you for the knowledge of Your presence
    with us all,
We thank You that You granted us to hear the
    Saviour's call.

We thank You, Lord, that You have given capacity
    to love,
We thank You for the partners whom You gave to
    share that love,
We thank You for the comfort given by each in
    troubled days,
We thank you for the sharing as we walk in Jesu's
    ways.

We thank You for the children You entrusted to
  our care,
We thank You for the wonder as we watched them
  lying there,
We thank You that where'er they go, You never
  leave their side,
We thank You and remember, Lord, Your love is
  deep and wide.

So now we come to worship You who share our
  sharing years,
Who blesses loving partnerships through
  laughter and through tears,
For joys of good companionship throughout Your
  ordained days,
We join our voices, hearts as one, to sing eternal
  praise.

O G Burchill,
Pewsey, Wiltshire

11
A friend of ours

Tune: Dundee (French)

Do not reject me now that I am old
(*Psalm 71:9*)

Why should I charge my soul with care?
The wealth in every mine
Belongs to Christ, God's Son and heir –
And He's a friend of mine!

The worries of retirement age –
Our income level dives!
The youngsters all have flown away,
But that's no cause to pine!

We have a friend, a heavenly friend,
And we hold evermore –
With Christ to guide us to the end –
The key to every door.

He loves the little tiniest tot,
And wildest, long-haired lad,
He says to us 'Forbid them not',
If we would make Him glad.

Rock gospel music, with its beat
Can make the young folk shine,
It makes them want to tap their feet,
And praise that friend of mine.

But when we elders want to sing
And raise our voice in praise
We like the dear belovèd hymns,
Known from the good old days.

Oh praise our friend, our precious friend,
And sing out loud and clear,
If hymns be old or new, who cares?
So long as we're sincere!

Richard MacDonald,
Bideford, Devon
(Richard was 82 when he wrote this hymn.)

12
Harvest Hymn

Tune: Amazing Grace

By Him we cry 'Abba, Father.' the Spirit
Himself testifies with our spirit that we
are God's children.

(Romans 8:15, NIV)

> *Abba, Abba, Abba, Abba,*
> *Abba, Abba, Abba.*

O Lord, all our endeavours have
By You been blessed tenfold,
The shining sun, high in the sky,
Shines on the harvest hold.
> *Abba, Abba . . .*

The cattle quietly grazing by
In soft green grass so lush,
The bird's sweet song in shaded tree
And sheep dot autumn's hush.
Abba, Abba . . .

The sheaves and fruits of tree and earth
Are safely gathered in.
We give you thanks, O Lord our God,
As winter's days begin.
Abba, Abba . . .

Mary Hudson,
Helensburgh, Dumbartonshire

Acknowledgements

Help the Aged and HarperCollins would firstly like to thank the 120 readers of *Yours* and *The Reader* who submitted almost 200 new hymns for use on National Sunday for Elderly People.

Sadly it was not possible to present them all in this edition of *Sing with Praise* and Thora has been placed in a very difficult position deciding on the 45 – the work of 31 writers – which it has been possible to include.

Thanks must be expressed to Lorraine Finn who typed all the hymns submitted. John Atkins, a choirmaster and organist in the diocese of Chichester has also to be thanked for musical editing. Major David Dalziel and his colleagues at the Salvation Army Headquarters made numerous valuable suggestions before the work finally went to press. And lastly Giles Semper and Roz Webber at HarperCollins are to be thanked for their professional assistance with the production.